THEN & NOW

HERNDON

OPPOSITE: Herndon, Virginia, a small station on the railroad linking Washington, DC, and western points of Virginia, became a focal point for growth as the Civil War ended and dairy farming expanded. The steam engine and her crew are shown at the Herndon Depot around 1910. (J. Berkley Green Collection, Herndon Historical Society.)

THEN & NOW

HERNDON

Laura Reasoner Jones

In honor of J. Berkley Green, whose foresight in preserving historic photographs made this possible. You are greatly missed.

Library of Congress Control Number: 2011921998

Published by Arcadia Publishing
Charleston, South Carolina

Printed in the United States of America

For all general information, please contact Arcadia Publishing:
Telephone 843-853-2070
Fax 843-853-0044
E-mail sales@arcadiapublishing.com
For customer service and orders:
Toll-Free 1-888-313-2665

Visit us on the Internet at www.arcadiapublishing.com

ON THE FRONT COVER: The Herndon Depot pictures epitomize the small town in its development over time. The depot has been restored to house a visitors' center and depot museum. The photograph below shows the depot in its heyday around 1907, when daily train service took passengers and freight to and from Washington, DC. (Then image courtesy of J. Berkley Green Collection, Herndon Historical Society; Now image courtesy of Laura Reasoner Jones.)

ON THE BACK COVER: The depot is partially hidden by the substation built in 1912 to provide power for the electric trains that connected Herndon and points west. (J. Berkley Green Collection, Herndon Historical Society.)

CONTENTS

Acknowledgments   vii

Introduction   ix

1.   Roads, Runs, and Railroads   11

2.   Resourcefulness   33

3.   Reading, Writing, and Reverence   49

4.   Resort Living   67

5.   Residents   73

6.   Rural Life   89

ACKNOWLEDGMENTS

Grateful thanks to the Herndon Historical Society, especially Carol Bruce and Virginia Clarity; to the staff in the Virginia Room of the Fairfax County Public Library, especially Suzanne Levy; and to Charles Mauro and Margaret Peck for their sublime earlier books about Herndon and its history.

As always, deep love and gratitude to Dennis Jones, whose camera and protection on those bridge-seeking trips keep me whole and relatively undamaged, and to my own two contributions to history—Christiana and Julie—remember, never sell the dead people!

All Then photographs are courtesy of the J. Berkley Green Collection, Herndon Historical Society unless otherwise noted. All Now photographs are courtesy of Laura Reasoner Jones.

INTRODUCTION

Herndon's tobacco-rolling roads and Indian trails are sunken today under the car-choked streets; its storied past is hidden to the casual visitor, who may only note a beautifully restored home or remark on an unusual street name. But Herndon is much more than a high-tech suburb of Washington, DC; more than home to multinational companies and multicultural residents. It is a town with a deep and vibrant history and with conflicts and stories playing out even today.

Formally established in 1858 with a post office in the railroad depot of the Alexandria, Loudoun, and Hampshire line, Herndon was named for a Virginia naval hero, Capt. William Lewis Herndon. Captain Herndon went down with his ship—the *Central America*, which carried a cargo of gold and hundreds of passengers—in a storm off Cape Hatteras in 1857. The town named for him was incorporated in 1879, comprising about four and a half square miles in western Fairfax County in the northernmost region of Virginia.

The town's acreage was split almost in two by the railroad line, and it had no sewers, paved streets, or electricity. However, Herndon did have 442 inhabitants, a school, three churches, five stores, two sawmills, a wheelwright, and other small businesses. It was poised for growth, though growth was slow in coming.

The land around Herndon was first populated by members of Paleo-Indian tribes who traveled up and down the East Coast. Artifacts from these and the later-arriving Archaic and Woodland Indians are still occasionally found in local excavations. The Dogue tribe, so named by Capt. John Smith and his party as they explored the Little Falls of the Potomac, were farming people who lived in small groups and villages along the local rivers and streams. The granting of Virginia land to several proprietors in 1649 and again in 1671 was the beginning of the end for these tribes, as the land was slowly sold or granted to settlers and speculators. The land where Herndon is located is but a small portion of the vast lands owned by Robert "King" Carter, member of the House of Burgesses and agent for Lord Fairfax.

Carter and his sons and other speculators hoped to find gold. They thought they had found copper, the next best thing, in a streambed south of the Herndon area. In order to ship this valuable commodity back to England, they built a road across Fairfax County to the Occoquan River wharves, thereby connecting this isolated outpost to the old world. But with the copper turning out to be valueless green sandstone, the area around what is now Herndon remained a wilderness with little population growth or settlement.

Loudoun County was carved out of the western portion of Fairfax County in 1757, with a new courthouse built in Leesburg for county residents. While the eastern part of Fairfax County burned with revolution, the forests around Herndon remained mostly untouched. In 1776, John Coleman built Elden House in the center of present-day Herndon on a 300-acre fruit farm. A small Primitive Baptist meetinghouse was built on Carter land and served as the only church in western Fairfax County until the Civil War.

On the northern side of Herndon, travelers were using the Vestal's Gap Road to travel west from Alexandria to the mountains. Taverns, or ordinaries, were reserved for their use, and the travelers frequented Coleman's Ordinary at the Sugarland Run ford. Over the years, as settlers and trade moved west, six different buildings at the Dranesville Tavern location hosted wayfarers along the Leesburg Turnpike from Alexandria to points west.

When building the railroad from Alexandria through Leesburg and Winchester, engineers chose the less costly route that passed directly through what is now the town of Herndon. The Alexandria, Loudoun & Hampshire Railroad established 16 station houses approximately three to three and a half miles apart. Herndon's station house was named Section 23 and was completed in 1857. A post office was established in 1858, necessitating a name for the town.

Herndon residents saw the soldiers crisscross the area during the Civil War. As a border state, residents were divided in their loyalties. One young woman, Laura Ratcliffe, aided Confederate lieutenant colonel John S. Mosby by providing information about Union troop movements. Another young Herndon woman, Kitty Kitchen, wrote of her experiences during Mosby's Raid in 1863, when her house was raided and her Union army guests were captured as prisoners of war.

After the war, growth came slowly but surely. Many Northerners moved to Fairfax County, utilizing the rebuilt railroad and contributing to the development of schools, churches, farms, and industry. Land was cheap and plentiful. After Herndon's incorporation in 1879, the town population grew slowly and steadily. It remained a farming community, however, and led the county in dairy production until World War II. The late 1950s brought the end of passenger service on the railroad, now the Washington & Old Dominion line, but freight service continued, as building supplies were needed for the construction of Dulles International Airport a few miles southwest of town. The last train ran in August 1968, and the railroad bed was converted to a bicycle trail, completed from Purcellville to Arlington in 1986.

Today, Herndon is both a destination and a commuter town with corporations and thriving businesses. With a population of over 21,000, it is an integral part of Fairfax County, contributing to educational achievement and cultural and historic attractions.

CHAPTER 1

ROADS, RUNS, AND RAILROADS

"Geography is destiny." Herndon's location along the Sugarland Run and the newly built railroad provided the ideal location for the growth of a town. This picture was taken around 1905, before fires and growth significantly altered the view looking east along the railroad. The depot and the Yellow House can be seen to the right of the tracks.

Mules and wagons were common sights in Herndon, even into the early 20th century. The local dairy farms used wagons and mules to transport milk from the western farms and the Floris area to the depot along the back road, now Monroe and Spring Streets. This wagon and driver are shown in front of Schneider's Hardware Store; no traces of the store remain now.

ROADS, RUNS, AND RAILROADS

Looking west on Elden Street along the unpaved roads of residential Herndon, most of these houses still remain well preserved or restored today. The first house on the right was originally the parsonage of the Methodist Episcopal church. Folly Lick Branch of the Sugarland Run crossed Elden Street at this location.

I.W. Cummings, deliveryman for Standard Oil, made deliveries using his horse and wagon. The Standard Oil facility was located where the municipal parking lot is today, near its intersection with Station Street. This is the scene of the highly anticipated Herndon Festival every June.

ROADS, RUNS, AND RAILROADS

Looking east on Elden Street toward the center of Herndon, the steeple of the former Episcopal church still stands tall, with the former manse across Grace Street now a family home. The former church building is now home to the Masonic lodge.

One block north of the Depot Square, Pine Street held many of the town's successful businesses, including Robey's Drugstore and Oliver's Shoe Store. These buildings, along with the private homes along Pine Street, were all destroyed in the fire of 1917. The office buildings on the right were built on the site of the Congregational church.

ROADS, RUNS, AND RAILROADS

Sugarland Run, a tributary of the Potomac River, was an essential geographic feature contributing to the development of western Fairfax County. The old Vestal's Gap Road and the later Leesburg Turnpike both required a ford at this site. Today the ford is part of the Stream Valley Park Trail for hikers.

A Quiet Spot

Near STERLING, VA.

Sterling, formerly Guilford, the next town west on the railroad, also enjoyed the beauty of small runs and streams. The Herndon area abounded with these runs, which contributed to the success of the numerous farms in the area. Many streams are underground now or surrounded by buildings, but small pockets of open land remain unspoiled.

ROADS, RUNS, AND RAILROADS

Road and railroad bridges over the many streams and runs were constructed out of the native Virginia clay, making sturdy bridges that have lasted until the present. This bridge is not visible from the surface roads today but is a landmark on the Washington & Old Dominion Trail as it crosses the Fairfax County Parkway at Spring Street.

Sugarland Run flows under the Old Dranesville Bridge on Leesburg Turnpike near the original ford, which was in use since the 1700s. Remnants of this bridge are present but difficult to find, as the six-lane Leesburg Turnpike intersects with the busy Fairfax County Parkway.

ROADS, RUNS, AND RAILROADS

Though it was still unpaved in 1905, Monroe Street on the eastern side of town became a fashionable street, with large, beautiful homes. The house on the left still stands today at the intersection of Monroe and Madison Streets.

Dranesville Auto Service stands today on Leesburg Turnpike in the building that originally housed W.O. Harrison's General Merchandise store. This area, called Herndon Junction, was a stop for travelers on their journey to and from Alexandria, Leesburg, and the Shenandoah Valley. (Then image courtesy of Great Falls Historical Society.)

ROADS, RUNS, AND RAILROADS

Griffith Hopkins's 1878 *Atlas of Fifteen Miles around Washington* notes ownership of land by Herndon residents—Barker, Crounse, Hanna, and Bready, to name a few. Parcels were large and undeveloped as compared to today's satellite view of Herndon. (Then image courtesy of the Fairfax Public Library; Now image courtesy of the Town of Herndon.)

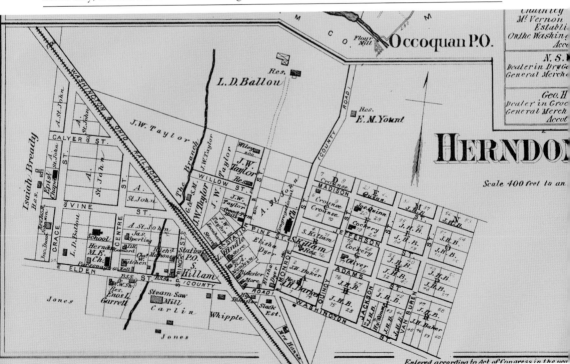

Looking down Station Street toward the depot, the building on the left had many tenants until it burned in the 1980s. This photograph was taken in the early 1900s. The depot still stands, a landmark for downtown Herndon.

Looking north on Station Street away from the depot, the one-story white building on the right sold harnesses and feed and tack supplies. The three-story office building replaced a service station and houses the Russia House Restaurant, open since 1992.

ROADS, RUNS, AND RAILROADS

Excitement and pride ran high in Herndon when the road from Floris was paved in 1903, making it easier for farmers to transport milk and dairy products to the Herndon Depot for daily shipment to Washington. The remaining sections of the roads connecting Herndon to the main Washington and Fairfax roads were not paved until the 1920s.

Before 1912, Herndon's business district was primarily north of the depot down Station Street to Pine Street. The town hall was built to the south (left) of the depot in 1939 as a project of the Works Progress Administration. For a time, it housed the post office and the jail in addition to all of the town's offices.

The route for the railroad line built in 1858 changed little over the years. Travel brochures for the Northern Virginia railroads boasted of "rolling hills and undulating valleys," and these were traversed by the trains and tourists as they headed west to cooler venues. The Washington & Old Dominion Hike and Bike Trail, one of the nation's most popular trails, follows the original train route.

Milk trains passed through Herndon twice daily, picking up full cans in the morning for processing and delivery in Washington, DC, and returning the previous day's cans in the evening. The cans and the passengers shared the loading platform. At one point, Fairfax County had the highest dairy production numbers in the commonwealth of Virginia. In 1916, Herndon had 19 milk shippers and 21 farmers. Fresh milk was advertised as one of the amenities of living in Herndon.

ROADS, RUNS, AND RAILROADS

The Herndon substation was built in 1912 to provide power to the newly electrified trains, blocking the eastern end of the depot. The Washington & Old Dominion substation was torn down in late 1969 when train service was discontinued. Today the depot serves as the centerpiece of the town square, with holiday celebrations in front of the town hall.

ROADS, RUNS, AND RAILROADS

In the 1960s, Herndon Depot was abandoned. After a brief period of activity transporting materials for the construction of Dulles Airport, the trains stopped in 1968, and the electric substation was torn down in 1969. But revitalization efforts led by townspeople and the Herndon Historical Society saved the depot from demolition. It has now been restored as a visitors' center and depot museum. (Then image courtesy of the Fairfax County Public Library.)

The Huddleson and Crippen buildings, farther up Station Street, burned in the fire of 1917, adding to the need for renewal. The fire spurred rebuilding efforts in Herndon's downtown, and the three-block area that burned was quickly repaired and restored. (Then image courtesy of the Fairfax County Public Library.)

CHAPTER 2

RESOURCEFULNESS

Small towns must have a core of services and businesses to thrive, and Herndon residents supported these and more. Without a courthouse as a focal point, Herndon's main business square began near the railroad depot—a fitting spot, as the railroad was the original reason for the town's existence. This photograph was taken shortly after 1912.

Dr. Edwin Detwiler came to Herndon from Pennsylvania. His office on Pine Street was unique for the time in that it was separate from his home. He installed a telephone on his porch in 1897; patients could call his home if he was not in his office. His charming office stands today, home of Brushstrokes, a hair and nail spa and salon.

RESOURCEFULNESS

Pete Simms was the only African American business owner in Herndon in the 1920s and 1930s. His blacksmith shop was located on Elden Street near J.J. Darlington's estate. Residents remember Simms making rings out of horseshoe nails for the neighborhood children. Jiffy Lube stands at this location today.

"Smithy"

The view from across the railroad tracks in the 1920s shows buildings that still stand and structures that have been demolished. The Nachman Building, on the right behind the trees, and the second building from the left remain in today's Herndon.

RESOURCEFULNESS

The National Bank of Herndon opened on Station Street in 1910. Closed briefly in 1935 for an investigation of fraud, it reopened as Citizen's National Bank. The beautifully restored building currently houses a physical coaching facility.

As visitors alighted from the train at the depot, they could see the age and charm of Herndon down Station Street. On the left were the Lowery Tea Room and the former Taylor Jewelry store, now Cushman Insurance Agency and Maude Hair Salon.

Wilkins and Bro. general store opened on the corner of Elden and Station Streets in 1897. This general store sold food, dry goods, and supplies to the town and surrounding areas. Two successful businesses are in this building today: Jimmy's Old Town Tavern and Roaches in the Attic Antiques.

Shown in 1959, the Esso station stood at the intersection of Dranesville Road and Leesburg Turnpike (Route 7) at Herndon Junction near the Sugarland Run ford and the old village of Dranesville. This area remained undeveloped until the mid-1970s when houses were built nearby and the roads were widened. (Then image courtesy of the Fairfax County Public Library.)

RESOURCEFULNESS

Herndon's first telephone company was partially financed by the Detwiler brothers, who needed phone service for their medical practices. The Chesapeake & Potomac Telephone Company (C&P) established an office for the town in 1916; the office burned in the 1917 fire but was immediately repaired and service restored. In the 1950s, C&P's office was on Pine Street; the Victorian building is now occupied by the Herndon Clock and Watch shop. (Then image courtesy of the Fairfax County Public Library.)

The Larro mill and Starlight Room dance hall were located in this large, partially vacant building until 1971 when the mill burned. Another burned-out building, the Pet and Hobby Shop, is out of sight to the right. Herndon's downtown suffered many devastating fires during its early days, necessitating much rebuilding. Herndon's town green is bordered by this land with the hike-and-bike trail on the former railroad bed, the new Herndon Fortnightly Library building, and the municipal center opened in the mid-1990s. The town green is home to a popular summer concert series, the annual Jazz Festival, the Veterans' Memorial, and the Peace Pole.

Herndon remained a rural community until the 1970s, when the Herndon Farm and Garden Center served the surrounding farms and their residents. This building, previously Dudding's Hardware and D&B Rentals, burned and was demolished in 1980. (Then image courtesy of the Fairfax County Public Library.)

Farmers drove their produce to the Herndon Packing House to be prepared for shipment to restaurants in Washington, DC. The packinghouse was conveniently located next to the railroad tracks at Center and Vine Streets. This location later housed the Humme and Robinson Mill and, later still, was home to International Harvester.

In the early 1920s, travelers disembarking from trains would first see a small town square with Dudding's Hardware Store, Nachman's Clothing Store, and the Herndon Hotel with 20 rooms for rent by the day, week, or month. The hotel also housed a news agency and a barbershop. It was later converted to apartments before being torn down in 1965.

Down Station Street, buildings were rebuilt and constructed after the devastation of the 1917 fire. Yount's Ford dealership is on the left. Harrison's Garage, the building in the center of the picture, is now the Closet, a nonprofit community thrift shop.

RESOURCEFULNESS

The Walker Building at the corner of Pine and Station Streets was the largest building in Fairfax County when it was destroyed in the fire of 1917. The fire also destroyed the subscription library owned by the Herndon Fortnightly Club. The replacement building became home to the A&P, the Tortilla Factory, and Zeffirelli, an Italian restaurant.

Harrison's garage was one of the town's livery stables, a mainstay for Herndon residents before they transitioned from a horse-drawn life. The Harrison stable changed with the times after the fire of 1917, evolving into a successful garage. The building then housed Perfection Automotive until 2000, when it was purchased by the Closet.

READING, WRITING, AND REVERENCE

Herndon grew up around schools and houses of worship. Floris, the small community to the west of Herndon, sent its white students to this school. A larger building was built in 1911, and this structure was moved to the Great Falls Grange to enlarge the Forestville Schoolhouse. Draft horses and wagon wheels moved the school 12 miles up Dranesville Road to its new home. (Courtesy of the Fairfax County Public Library.)

Built in 1873 as Herndon's first public school, this small building on Center Street originally had only one room. It was expanded to two and then three rooms by 1912, when the town built a larger school for grades 1 through 12 on Locust Street. It is now a private home.

Mary Lee Castleman, cousin of Robert E. Lee, established the Herndon Female Seminary in her home in 1876. This school accepted girl boarders and boys under 12 until the mid-1920s. Built in 1868, the house has undergone many restorations and renovations. Souvenirs of the former students have been found in the attic.

Herndon's new school opened in 1912, drawing white students in grades 1 through 12 from the town and surrounding farms. Enough land was purchased from the original Eldenwood Fruit Farm acreage to build sports fields and multiple outbuildings to train students in agriculture, business, and home economics. Herndon High School had the first cafeteria in Fairfax County. This building burned and was replaced in 1928. A cannery for farm produce operated here until the 1990s. This is now the site of Herndon Middle School.

READING, WRITING, AND REVERENCE

Oak Grove elementary school served African American students from two neighborhoods in Herndon. Students walked or traveled by train. This building was erected in the 1950s, consolidating three schools for African American children. The county schools were desegregated in 1965, and all students began attending their neighborhood schools. This building is now owned by the Town of Herndon and is used by the Herndon Department of Public Works.

African American students around Herndon traveled long distances to their segregated schools. One such school, at the end of Squirrel Hill Road on the grounds of the Mount Pleasant Baptist Church, burned in the 1940s. Older students desiring higher education traveled by bus to Manassas, about 20 miles away.

In 1923, students at the Floris School celebrated spring with a maypole dance. Notice the open farmland surrounding the school. Today, students at McNair Elementary, built on the site of one of Herndon's largest dairy farms, play with a parachute during their annual spring Field Day.

Frying Pan Spring Meetinghouse dates back to 1783, when it was on the preaching circuit for the Primitive Baptist Church. The building was in continuous operation from 1775 until 1964, when it was deeded to the Fairfax County Park Authority for restoration and preservation. Racially integrated since its inception, the meetinghouse sheltered injured soldiers as Confederate brigadier general J.E.B. Stuart's troops roamed the area.

READING, WRITING, AND REVERENCE

The Herndon Congregational Church at the corner of Monroe and Pine Streets was organized in 1868, and the building was dedicated in 1875. The congregation merged with the Herndon Presbyterian Church and then the Floris Presbyterian Church, forming Trinity Presbyterian Church in 1959. Photographed in 1907, this building was saved by dynamiting the neighboring buildings in the fire of 1917. Office buildings are located on this site today.

The original St. Timothy's Episcopal Church began as a mission church in 1868. The lot on Elden Street was purchased for $60 in 1876, and this building was consecrated in 1881. It was used by the growing congregation until 1969, when they moved to a larger building on Van Buren Street. Herndon's Masonic Lodge No. 264 purchased the building at that time.

READING, WRITING, AND REVERENCE

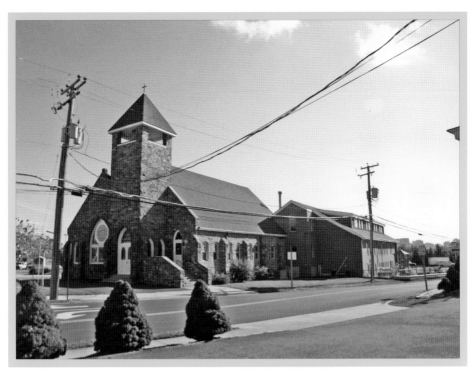

Built and dedicated in 1900, the First Baptist Church was constructed on land donated by J.J. Darlington, one of Herndon's wealthiest residents. This picture, taken in the 1920s or 1930s, shows the grove of trees behind the church where Darlington's large house and grounds were located. The church was constructed with stone from the quarry located on Darlington's property.

Organized in 1866 in the old Floris School, Mount Pleasant Baptist Church relocated to this building on Horsepen Road, now Coppermine Road, in 1882. That small building is now home to another congregation, while the Mount Pleasant congregation built a larger church facility on nearby Squirrel Hill Road in 1999.

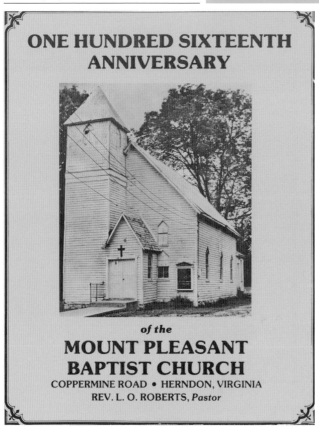

ONE HUNDRED SIXTEENTH ANNIVERSARY

of the

MOUNT PLEASANT BAPTIST CHURCH

COPPERMINE ROAD • HERNDON, VIRGINIA

REV. L. O. ROBERTS, *Pastor*

Prior to 1797, colonists were worshipping at the Sugarland Chapel on the highest point of the Coleman land near the community of Dranesville on Leesburg Turnpike. In 1833, James Coleman donated land for the use of Liberty Church. During the Civil War, a skirmish was fought around the church, and the buildings were used as a hospital and stable.

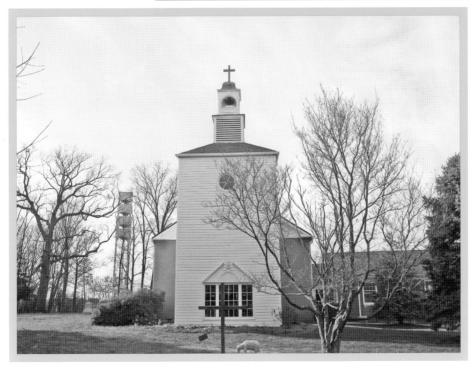

Located in a wooded area off Sterling Road, Oak Grove Baptist Church was founded in 1868. The train stopped at Oak Grove, allowing worshippers to attend services. This building burned in 1957 but was rebuilt. The fifth building on this site was opened in 2000. An old cemetery shelters former members.

READING, WRITING, AND REVERENCE

Herndon's Northern Methodist Church was built on Elden Street in 1872. It was used until 1939 when the congregation united with the Southern Methodist Church and began using the larger building constructed in 1915 on Spring Street. Now home to Iglesias de Dios Pentecostal El Calvario, the Spring Street building housed the united congregations until 1987, when they built a larger facility on Bennett Street.

First Presbyterian Church of Herndon used this building on Jefferson Street until it merged with the Congregational Church in 1949. It later merged with Floris Presbyterian Church and formed Trinity Presbyterian Church. This building is now a private residence.

St. Joseph's Roman Catholic Mission Parish was established in 1923, and this small stone building was dedicated in 1926. The congregation outgrew this space and moved to its current location on Peachtree Street in 1964. This building is now occupied by HRI, a local insurance business.

As Herndon grew, the need for a central cemetery became apparent. Herndon residents came together and purchased a large tract of land in 1874 to be developed as a town cemetery. Platted by 1882, Chestnut Grove Cemetery became a favorite Sunday afternoon walk for the growing town. It now contains more than 25 acres.

READING, WRITING, AND REVERENCE

CHAPTER 4

RESORT LIVING

Mr. J. J. Darlington's
Residence,
Herndon, Va.

Trains from Washington, DC, brought visitors looking for cooler summer residences west. One such visitor, J.J. Darlington, bought a Victorian home and nine acres of land in an oak grove in Herndon and brought his family and servants to summer in 1891. He bought and farmed over 500 acres, including a stone quarry and a swimming hole on Sugarland Run.

Darlington Grove became a focal point for prominent Washingtonians attending summer house parties and barbecues with hundreds of guests. J.J. Darlington's guests included the ambassador from Korea and his family. Herndon residents marveled at the exotic guests. In 1910, Brig. Gen. John S. Mosby's men held a reunion at Darlington Grove, retelling war stories and reliving the glory of their battles. The land was sold over the years and now is covered with office and retail buildings.

rover's Rest
Dranesville Tavern
Dranesville, Virginia

Of the five taverns located along Sugarland Run and Leesburg Turnpike, the surviving Dranesville Tavern was host to casual travelers and drovers herding sheep and cattle between the port of Alexandria and the Shenandoah Valley. The tavern was acquired by the Fairfax County Park Authority in 1968 and moved 100 feet south to accommodate expansion of the Leesburg Turnpike. Under the clapboard siding, there are three log structures connected with dogtrot passageways.

Currently the location of the planned community of Reston, Thornton Station was one stop east of Herndon. Dr Carl Wiehle bought 3,500 acres at this location in 1886 to establish a resort community and town. Visitors paid $30 per month for room and board to stay in the 35-room Aesculapius Hotel during the 1890s, but the building lots did not sell, and Wiehle died impoverished in 1901.

The gazebo on the Wiehle grounds was built over the springhouse that provided water for the Wiehle family in their manor house, which was completed in 1902 after Wiehle's death. During the resort's heyday, a wooden footbridge connected the train station with the gazebo. Four hand-dug lakes were originally part of the resort planned by Wiehle; they were drained each summer and re-dug to their eight-foot depth.

The Wiehle family remained on the main property, selling off land to the Hutchison family and, later, the Bowman family for their distillery, which operated until the early 1960s when the acreage became the planned community of Reston. In this photograph, the Wiehle summer home and the town social hall/church can be seen, with the white clapboard house at the right, a model for Wiehle's failed planned community.

RESIDENTS

Abner Baker Home — Herndon, Va.

As Herndon grew in the late 1800s, farmers and merchants built large houses for burgeoning families. Abner and Betsy Baker lived on a farm on the western edge of Herndon, land that is now covered with hotel and retail development.

One of Herndon's first teachers, William Sweetser, lived on Station Street near its intersection with Pine Street. Sweetser was also one of the members of the first town council, which was sworn in on February 8, 1879. His home held the post office, and he was one of Herndon's first postmasters. Today Dominion Animal Hospital stands on this site.

The Wrenn family lived in Herndon before 1880, serving the town in many capacities. Raymond Wrenn, a real estate agent, was elected mayor in 1920. Additions have been made to this house, but it stands beautifully preserved today on Station Street.

Home of Herndon's undertaker Thomas Reed, the Yellow House was built before 1874. At one time a school, the house was moved twice: first in 1920 to 719 Elden Street when Reed built the brick house next door for the current Adams-Green Funeral Home and again in 2006, when it was purchased for preservation.

Wilson and Virginia Nickell McNair raised their family in this farmhouse on their large dairy farm on the southern edge of Herndon off Centreville Road. Herndon residents fondly remember picnics and hayrides on the McNair land. The family sold the land in the early 1990s; no traces remain of the farm today, other than the school and shopping center named in honor of the McNairs.

Built in 1911 and called the Summit, Edwin Detwiler's medical office still stands today on one of Herndon's highest points. Detwiler and his brother Benjamin served Herndon as physician and dentist from 1887 until 1916, when Edwin was murdered by a mentally ill patient. This building still serves as an office.

RESIDENTS

Hopkins's 1878 Atlas placed Ephraim Yount's house on the edge of Herndon's town limits. Yount, a government employee, lived with his wife, Laura Musselman, on what is now Monroe Street. The land is currently slated for development, but the house will be moved and preserved.

Isaiah Bready moved from New York in 1847, building a small house near Main and Vine Streets. A scout in the Union army, he later built this large home, called Elwardstone, on Vine Street. Isaiah Bready was elected the first mayor of Herndon in 1879. Bready descendants still live in this home today.

Sitting on a rise on Monroe Street, this home was built after the Civil War by Amos Crounse, a Union veteran who remained in Virginia after the war. The Crounse family owned land in all sections of Herndon. One of the oldest trees in Herndon grew on this land until 2009, when it was toppled during a severe storm.

Another old family home still stands on Elden Street, Herndon's main thoroughfare. This house was built around 1870 for the Ballou family and was home for a time to Gen. William Urich, a Civil War veteran and town council member. The wraparound porch was added after 2000.

The western boundary of Herndon was home to this beautiful farmhouse where local children picked beans and berries as late as the 1930s and 1940s. The land and home were sold as Herndon grew, and the Verizon office now stands in its place. (Then image courtesy of the Fairfax County Public Library.)

Originally the parsonage for the First Baptist Church, this large farmhouse has been home to many families over the years. Barbara Harding, a retired schoolteacher, raised her family and operated Harding Hall, a day care center. This home has nurtured many young Herndon children over the years.

The Barker family owned land in Herndon and contributed to its social and intellectual life. Their home, located in a grove of pine trees near Elden and Monroe Streets, was torn down before 1978 to make way for the Pines Shopping Center. Residents recalled the lovely sound of the pine trees on summer evenings.

Dr. Benjamin Detwiler, Herndon's prominent dentist, built his home on Elden Street on land originally part of the Eldenwood Fruit Farm. He and his brother Edwin also started the Herndon Gas Company. The only remaining privately owned gashouse in town is behind his former home today.

Now called Merrybrook, this home just west of the Herndon town limits belonged to Milton Hanna and his wife, Laura Ratcliffe, who was well known locally for providing information on troop movements to Brig. Gen. John S. Mosby and Gen. J.E.B. Stuart during the Civil War. Merrybrook remains in danger of destruction as building goes on all around it. It is in the National Register of Historic Places and is the last remaining historic structure on Centreville Road.

Col. John Coleman, a Revolutionary War officer, built Elden House on 300 acres near the current intersection of Locust and Center Streets around 1776. Land was divided and sold for Herndon's original high school and for apartments. The remaining house buildings were torn down in 1964. Reminders of this time exist only in an overgrown Coleman family cemetery behind the middle school.

RURAL LIFE

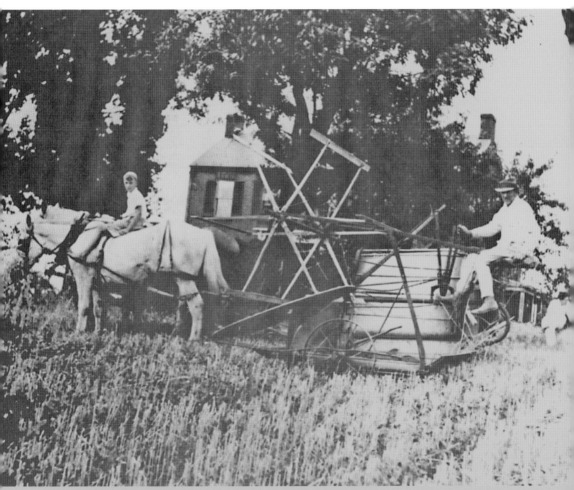

At the core of Fairfax County's dairy industry, Herndon's railroad service allowed milk to be delivered safely to the many dairy processing plants in and around the Washington, DC, area. Other types of farming thrived also, as evidenced in this photograph of a bumper wheat crop from the 1930s. That life is gone now, with only 10 acres currently in use for farming around Herndon and none within the town limits.

Kidwell Farm, at Frying Pan Park on the western edge of Herndon, preserves Fairfax County's rural heritage as a working family farm. The farm is home to chickens, draft horses, cows, sheep, goats, and pigs. Originally a dairy operation, Kidwell Farm provides a snapshot of family farming from the 1920s to 1940s for Fairfax County's highly urban families. (Then image courtesy of the Fairfax County Public Library.)

Joseph Moffett's blacksmith shop was a core business in downtown Herndon, serving the needs of Herndon's equine residents. It burned in the 1917 fire but was rebuilt immediately. The shop evolved into wagon and auto repair and sold farm supplies until it closed in 1955. The blacksmith shop was moved to Frying Pan Park in 1975, and the foundations remain in the heart of town next to one of the two remaining gashouses restored by the Herndon Historical Society.

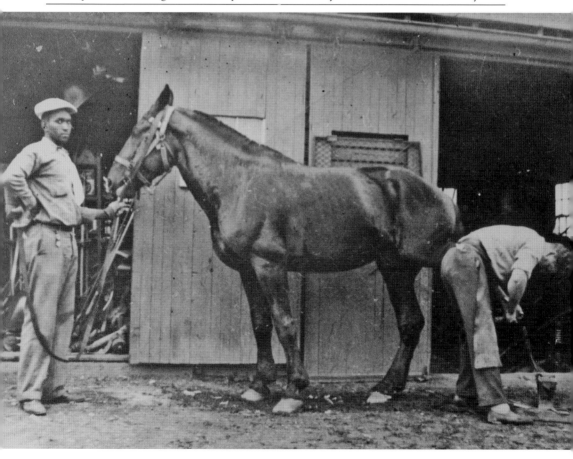

Covered now with office parks and Herndon Post Office property, the land along the path of Coral Road was once home to family farms. The Wiley house was the last one standing on Coral Road. It was demolished in 1998 as offices were built along Spring Street. Coral Road is no longer a street; it has been annexed by the Washington & Old Dominion trail.

The next stop west on the railroad was Guilford, now Sterling, an old community along the Vestal's Gap Road. As in Herndon, large dairy farms were the rule. Sterling is now completely developed with the exception of small pockets of open space preserved for resident use.

Oat and wheat crops were tested in the rich fields around Herndon. This young boy stands in the Schaub fields at the dividing line between two oat crops treated with different fertilizers. With only a few acres of active farmland left around Herndon, homes and buildings encroach daily. National and international companies, spurred by the opening of Dulles International Airport in 1962, have built headquarters all around Herndon, requiring housing for employees. (Then image courtesy of the Fairfax County Public Library.)

RURAL LIFE

To commemorate Herndon's railroad history, this caboose belonging to the Norfolk Southern Railway was donated to the town and painted in the livery of the Washington & Old Dominion line in 1989. It has become a symbol of Herndon's history, providing a colorful landmark for residents and visitors alike. The railroad built Herndon and lives on today in one of Herndon's favorite local attractions.

www.arcadiapublishing.com

Discover books about the town where you grew up, the cities where your friends and families live, the town where your parents met, or even that retirement spot you've been dreaming about. Our Web site provides history lovers with exclusive deals, advanced notification about new titles, e-mail alerts of author events, and much more.

MADE IN THE USA

Arcadia Publishing, the leading local history publisher in the United States, is committed to making history accessible and meaningful through publishing books that celebrate and preserve the heritage of America's people and places. Consistent with our mission to preserve history on a local level, this book was printed in South Carolina on American-made paper and manufactured entirely in the United States.

This book carries the accredited Forest Stewardship Council (FSC) label and is printed on 100 percent FSC-certified paper. Products carrying the FSC label are independently certified to assure consumers that they come from forests that are managed to meet the social, economic, and ecological needs of present and future generations.

FSC
Mixed Sources
Product group from well-managed
forests and other controlled sources

Cert no. SW-COC-001530
www.fsc.org
© 1996 Forest Stewardship Council

Find Your Place in History.